Let's COUNT EASTER

© Kids Book Design Co.

HOW MANY CHICKS ARE THERE?

THERE ARE 7 CHICKS

HOW MANY FLOWERS ARE THERE?

THERE ARE

5

FLOWERS

1
2
3
4
5

HOW MANY BASKETS ARE THERE?

THERE ARE

4

BASKETS

1

2

3

4

HOW MANY TULIPS ARE THERE?

THERE ARE

6

TULIPS

1
2
3
4
5
6

HOW MANY CROSSES ARE THERE?

THERE ARE

3

CROSSES

HOW MANY EGGS ARE THERE?

HOW MANY BUTTERFLIES ARE THERE?

THERE ARE

4

BUTTERFLIES

1

2

3

4

HOW MANY CARROTS ARE THERE?

THERE ARE

3

CARROTS

HOW MANY CANDIES ARE THERE?

THERE ARE

2

CANDIES

1

2

HOW MANY BUNNIES ARE THERE?

HOW MANY LADYBUGS ARE THERE?

THERE ARE 7 LADYBUGS

HOW MANY TROLLEYS ARE THERE?

THERE ARE

3

TROLLEYS

1

2

3

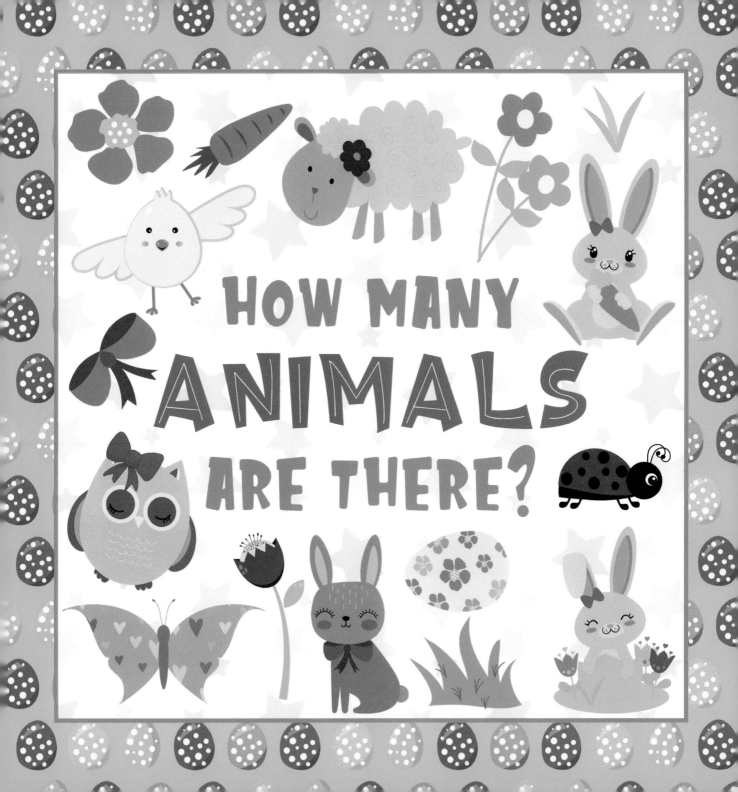

HOW MANY ANIMALS ARE THERE?

THERE ARE 8 ANIMALS

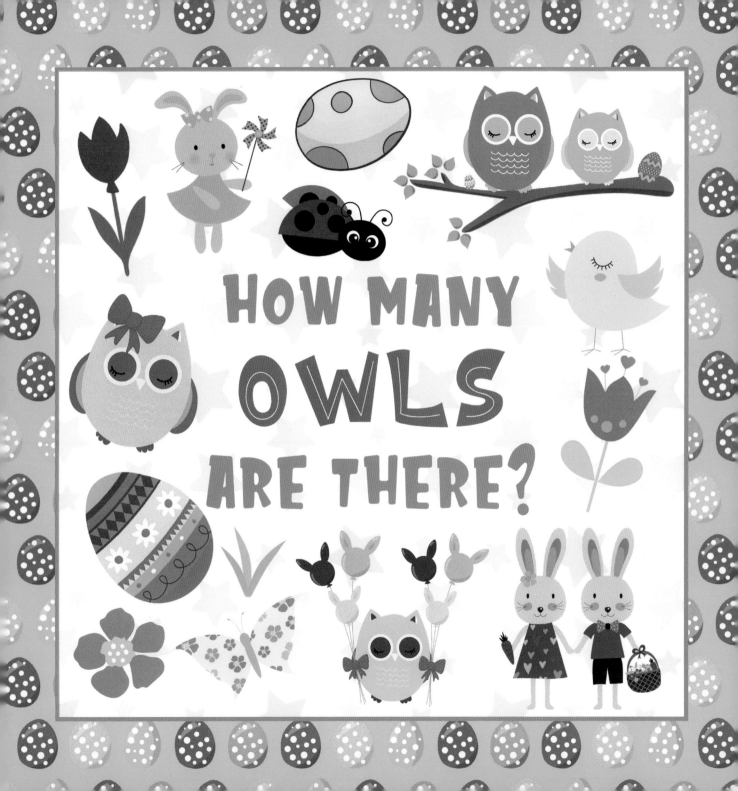

HOW MANY OWLS ARE THERE?

THERE ARE

4

OWLS

1
2
3
4

HOW MANY CHILDREN ARE THERE?

THERE ARE

2

CHILDREN

HOW MANY LAMBS ARE THERE?

THERE ARE

3

LAMBS

1

2

3

HOW MANY JELLY BEANS ARE THERE?

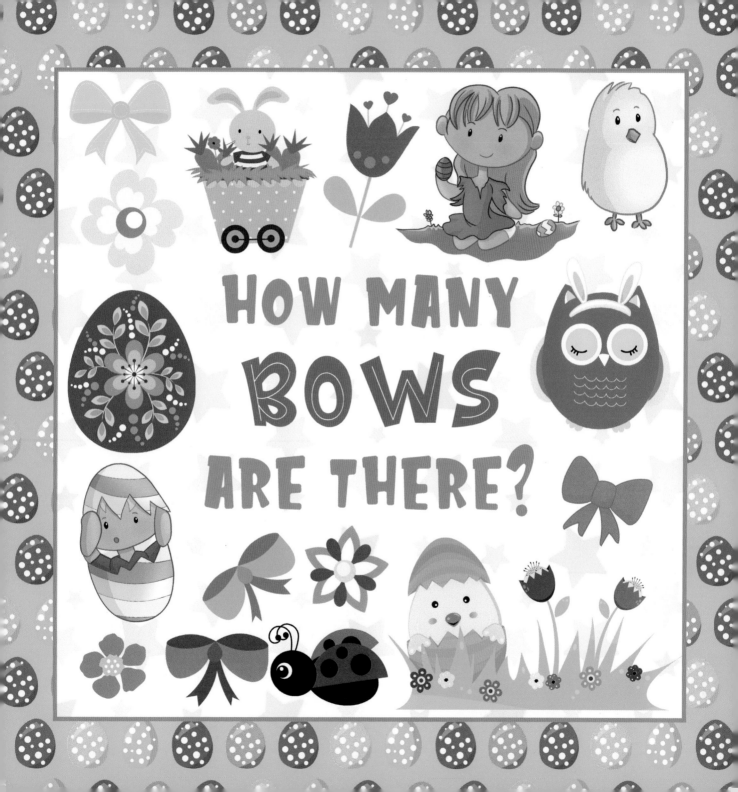

HOW MANY BOWS ARE THERE?

THERE ARE

4

BOWS

1

2

3

4

I hope you enjoyed this book!

Printed in Germany
by Amazon Distribution
GmbH, Leipzig

17300163R00023